LifeCycles

Pup to Shark

Camilla de la Bédoyère

QED Publishing

Words in **bold** are explained in the glossary on page 22.

Copyright © QED Publishing 2009

First published in the UK in 2009 by
QED Publishing
A Quarto Group company
226 City Road
London EC1V 2TT

www.qed-publishing.co.uk

A catalogue record for this book is available from
the British Library.

ISBN 978 1 84835 926 0

Printed in China

Author Camilla de la Bédoyère
Editor Angela Royston
Designer and Picture Researcher Melissa Alaverdy

Picture credits
(t=top, b=bottom, l=left, r=right, c=centre, fc=front cover)
Alamy 16 Visual&Written SL
Corbis 15c Visuals Unlimited, 15r Visuals Unlimited
Getty Images 15t Alex Kerstitch, 20–21 National Geographic
imagequestmarine.com 4–5 Masa Ushioda, 6–7 Masa
Ushioda, 15b Andy Murch/V&W
naturepl.com 6b Brandon Cole, 6t Doug Perrine, 8l Jeff
Rotman 10b Doug Perrine, 10t Doug Perrine, 11 Doug Perrine,
14 Jurgen Freund
NHPA 1t Oceans Image/Photoshot
Photolibrary Group 2t James Watt, 8–9 Reinhard Dirscherl,
12–13 David B Fleetham, 13t Richard Herrmann, 18–19 James
Watt, 19t Kelvin Aitken
Shutterstock 1b Naluphoto, 3t Mashvesna, 17t Stephan
Kerkhofs, 17b Ian Scott, 24b Ian Scott

Contents

What is a shark?

A shark is a kind of fish. Many fish have long, slender bodies. This shape is perfect for moving through water.

There are more than 400 types of shark in the world. Most of them are harmless to people, and feed on small animals in the sea.

Eye

Teeth

Sharks have **gill slits** on each side of their heads. They use them for breathing underwater.

⇩Sharks are excellent swimmers. Their fins help them to swim and to change direction.

Fin

Gill slits

The story of a shark

Young sharks are called **pups**.
All pups begin life as eggs.

Some sharks lay their eggs on
the **seabed** before they hatch.
The pups of some sharks grow
inside their mother's body
until they are born.

The story of how
pups grow into
adult sharks is
called a **life cycle**.

2

Pup

1

⇐ A lemon shark
has three stages
in its life cycle.

Pups grow from eggs
inside the mother

3

Adult shark

New lives begin

Before a female shark can have pups, she must **mate** with a male shark.

The male holds the female tight when they mate. He grabs her with special fins called claspers. The male may even bite the female during mating.

The male **fertilizes** the female's eggs. Only fertilized eggs can grow into new sharks.

⇧Only male sharks have fins called claspers.

Claspers

⇩When sharks mate, they wrap their bodies around each other.

Giving birth

The pups of lemon sharks grow from eggs inside their mother's body.

At first, a pup takes food from the egg **yolk**. It grows until it is big enough to **hatch** from the egg.

After it has hatched, the pup gets food from its mother's body.

⇨Female sharks find safe places to give birth. These places are called nurseries.

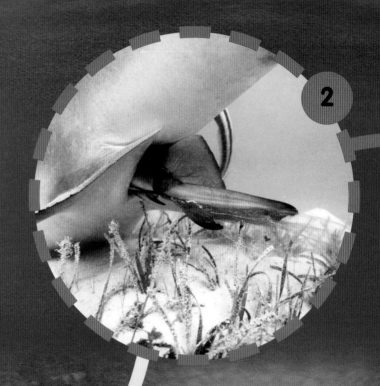

⇧As many as 17 pups may be born, one after the other.

The food passes from the mother to the pup through the **placenta**. After about a year, the pups are born.

⇩This newborn pup is still attached to its placenta.

3

Placenta

Hungry pups

Great white sharks also keep their growing pups inside their body.

A great white shark does not have a placenta. First, the pups take in food from the yolk.

When they hatch, the pups need to find more food. They eat any spare eggs, and they may even eat each other.

⇨ Great white sharks can grow up to 6 metres in length.

It takes about six years for a great white pup to grow into an adult.

As soon as the pups are born, the mother swims away. The pups have to survive by themselves.

Laying eggs

Swell sharks lay their eggs. The female finds a safe place for her eggs to grow.

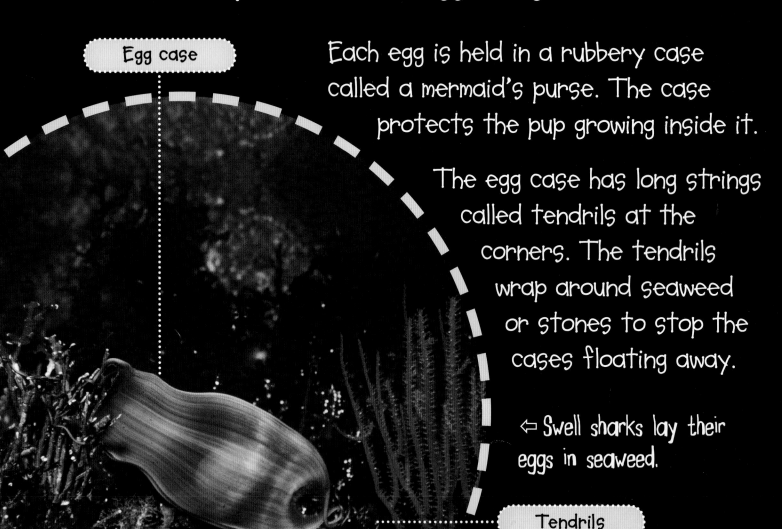

Egg case

Each egg is held in a rubbery case called a mermaid's purse. The case protects the pup growing inside it.

The egg case has long strings called tendrils at the corners. The tendrils wrap around seaweed or stones to stop the cases floating away.

⇐ Swell sharks lay their eggs in seaweed.

Tendrils

⇐Inside an egg case there is a tiny shark pup and white yolk.

⇨At three months old, the shark pup's tail has grown longer.

⇩After seven to ten months the swell shark pup is ready to hatch.

⇩An adult swell shark can grow up to one metre long.

1

2

3

4

Growing up

Not all pups grow into adults. Sometimes they are eaten by other animals. Even adult sharks eat pups.

Some pups are covered with patterns that help them to hide. This is called **camouflage**.

⇩ Swell sharks swim near the sea floor, where they are hard to see.

16

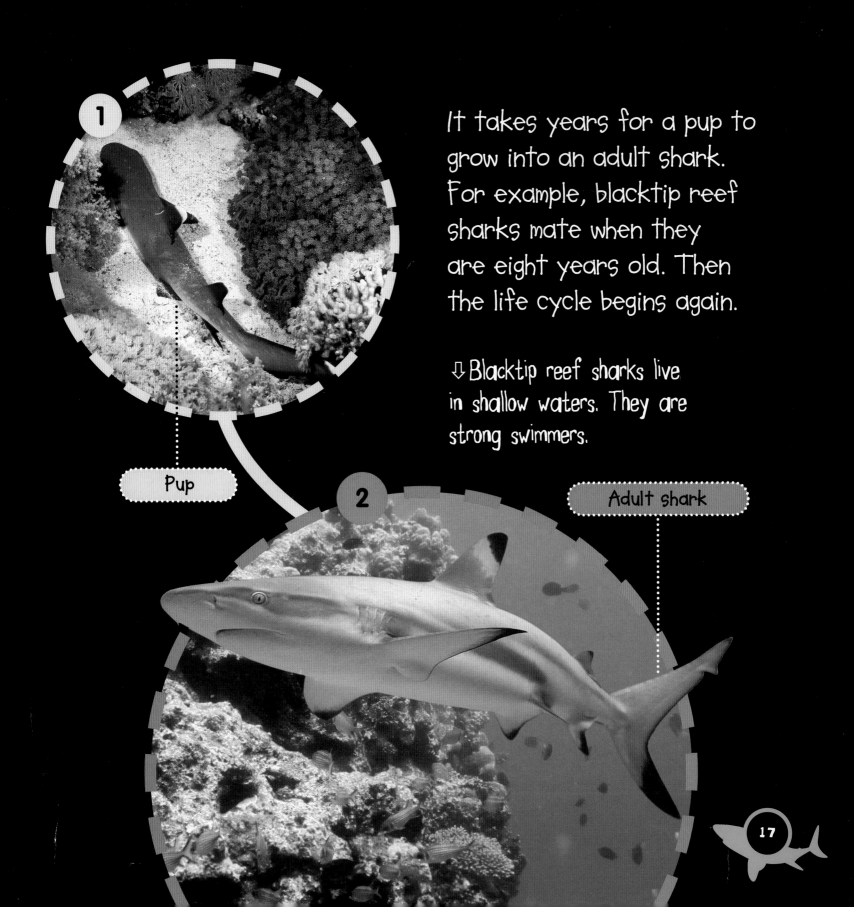

It takes years for a pup to grow into an adult shark. For example, blacktip reef sharks mate when they are eight years old. Then the life cycle begins again.

⇩ Blacktip reef sharks live in shallow waters. They are strong swimmers.

1

Pup

2

Adult shark

How sharks live

Sharks swim silently through the sea, searching for food to eat.

Great white sharks hunt seals and other fish. They attack with lightning speed and have teeth as sharp as razors.

Whale sharks wait for food to come to them. They keep their mouths open and swallow tiny **krill**.

⇧ Whale sharks are the largest fish in the world.

18

⇨Krill look like small shrimps. Each one is no bigger than your little finger!

Sharks in danger

Sharks have survived on Earth for hundreds of millions of years, but now they are in danger.

Every year, millions of sharks die. They are caught by accident in fishing nets, or they are hunted by people for food.

⇨ Hammerhead sharks have huge heads. They often get caught in nets.

It is possible that hammerhead sharks, great white sharks and many other types of shark will soon disappear forever.

Glossary

Camouflage
Patterns and colours that help an animal to hide.

Fertilize
When a special male cell joins with a female's egg so it can grow into a new living thing.

Gill slits
Parts of the body a fish uses to breathe underwater.

Hatch
When a pup breaks out of its egg.

Krill
Small animals that live in the sea and look like shrimps.

Life cycle
The story of how a living thing changes from birth to death and how it produces young.

Mate
When a male and female come together and a new life starts to grow.

Placenta
Part of a shark's egg joins with the mother's body to create a placenta. Food is passed to the growing pup through the placenta.

Pup
Young shark.

Seabed
The ground at the bottom of the sea. It is made of sand, mud, stones and rocks.

Yolk
Part of an egg that provides food for the growing pup.

22

Index

Notes for parents and teachers

- Look through the book and talk about the pictures. Read the captions and ask questions about other things in the photographs that have not been mentioned in the text.

- Help your child to find out more about one type of shark mentioned in this book. Use the Internet together to discover more about how it feeds and where it lives. Does it lay eggs, or does it give birth? Find out other interesting facts about the shark. Look on the Internet for photos of the shark and help your child to draw a picture of it.

- Exploring science. Visit an aquarium so you can watch how fish move through water. Talk about what makes one type of fish different from another type. Use words that describe the fish's body shape, size and colour. Find the largest and smallest fishes in the aquarium.

- Be prepared for questions about human life cycles. There are plenty of books for this age group that can help you give age-appropriate explanations.

- Talking about a child's family helps them to link life processes, such as reproduction, to their own experience. Drawing simple family trees, looking at photo albums and sharing family stories with grandparents are fun ways to engage young children.

24